CW01150381

Original title:
The Curious Case of Fluttering Feelings

Copyright © 2024 Creative Arts Management OÜ
All rights reserved.

Author: Jasper Montgomery
ISBN HARDBACK: 978-9916-90-760-3
ISBN PAPERBACK: 978-9916-90-761-0

The Illusion of Everlasting Moments

In the dawn's gentle light, we chase,
The fleeting shadows, time's soft embrace.
Whispers of laughter, echoes of dreams,
A tapestry woven with silken seams.

Yet hours slip by, like grains of sand,
Wishing to hold what we can't command.
Each smile a treasure, yet moments fade,
In the garden of life, memories are made.

Under starlit skies, we find our peace,
Moments of solace, a sweet release.
But like the tide, they ebb and flow,
Leaving behind what we long to know.

With every heartbeat, we grasp at air,
Chasing the seconds, a fruitless affair.
The illusion lingers, a shimmering ghost,
In the dance of time, we cherish the most.

Bewitched by the Fluttering Light

In the twilight's soft embrace,
Fireflies dance with gentle grace.
Their glow paints dreams on the night,
I am lost in the magic's light.

Each flicker whispers a sweet tune,
Underneath the silvered moon.
My heart flutters, caught in flight,
Bewitched by the shimmering sight.

Whims of the Heart in Motion

A gentle breeze stirs in the air,
Promises of love linger there.
With every heartbeat, we collide,
In the dance where dreams abide.

We twirl beneath the starry haze,
Lost in the warmth of tender gaze.
Our spirits soar, forever bright,
Boundless like the morning light.

Whispers of Unspoken Emotions

In silence, secrets softly bloom,
Filling the space, breaking the gloom.
Eyes meet in a knowing glance,
Unraveled threads of muted chance.

Words unsaid hang heavy in air,
Each heartbeat a silent prayer.
Emotions weave like threads of night,
Binding souls in whispered light.

A Symphony of Daring Hearts

In the rhythm of brave endeavors,
Hearts sing like unbroken rivers.
With courage stitched in every seam,
We chase the elusive dream.

A melody that dares to soar,
With beats that echo evermore.
Together, we reach for the stars,
Creating music from our scars.

The Dance of Unshed Tears

In shadows deep, the silence weeps,
A fragile waltz, where memory keeps.
With every glance, the heart will sway,
To melodies of what can't stay.

A gentle fall, like whispered sighs,
In hidden corners, where pain lies.
Each droplet glimmers in the light,
A dance of dusk, embracing night.

Yet through the gloom, a spark ignites,
Hope's tender glow in darkest sights.
In every tear a tale is spun,
A rhythm felt, though lost to fun.

So let them flow, these unshed streams,
For in their course, we weave our dreams.
The dance continues, bold and free,
A fragile strength, a symphony.

Fluttering Through Dreams

Beneath the stars, the visions rise,
Like whispers soft in twilight skies.
They flutter forth, on gentle breeze,
  A tapestry of hopes with ease.

Each dream a bird, on wings of light,
That dances through the velvet night.
In realms where thoughts are free to play,
They paint the dawn in shades of gray.

Amongst the trees, where shadows blend,
The heart takes flight, no need to mend.
For every dream will find its way,
In endless night or breaking day.

So float along, on currents warm,
Embrace the magic, feel the charm.
In dreams we find our truest part,
  A flight of joy, a beating heart.

Echoes of Affection on the Wind

In whispers soft, affection flows,
Carried by breezes, love bestows.
Each echo calls from far and near,
Reminders sweet, that hearts hold dear.

Through cedar trees and silver streams,
The wind weaves tales of silent dreams.
Each breath a promise, light as air,
Connecting souls with gentle care.

In the twilight, where shadows blend,
The echoes speak, they never end.
From mountains high to valleys low,
Love's whisper lingers, soft and slow.

So let the wind, with love, express,
The sweet refrain of happiness.
For in the echoes, truth we find,
A symphony of heart and mind.

Enigmas of a Shimmering Heart

A heart aglow with mystery,
Holds secrets deep, like history.
In shimmering light, it pulses slow,
An enigma wrapped in softest glow.

Each beat a riddle, softly sung,
With whispers of the young and sprung.
It dances lightly through the night,
Casting shadows, fragile light.

In moonlit silence, truths unfold,
A tapestry of tales retold.
With every pulse, the world reveals,
The hidden joys, the silent heals.

So cherish well these shimmering sparks,
For in their depths, love alwaysarks.
An enigma bright, forever light,
In every heart, a cherished sight.

Quicksilver Sentiments

In twilight's glow, we dance and sway,
Whispers of silver in night's ballet.
Hearts race swiftly, like a stream,
Fleeting moments, lost in a dream.

Eyes entwined, a spark ignites,
Timeless echoes in starry nights.
Words unspoken, feelings glow,
Quicksilver paths where passions flow.

A Serenade of Starlit Emotions

Beneath the stars, soft shadows play,
Melodies linger, in night's array.
A song of longing, sweet and clear,
Echoing softly, love draws near.

Hearts entwined in the moon's embrace,
Every glance a sacred space.
Songs of the night, gently unfold,
Tales of our love, forever told.

The Gentle Rise of Longing

Morning light waves a soft good day,
With every dawn, dreams drift away.
Yet in the quiet, desires bloom,
Yearning whispers through the room.

Each heartbeat speaks, a silent plea,
Longing grows like a whispered sea.
In gentle rise, the heart takes flight,
Carried softly on wings of light.

Fluttering Hues of Desire

Petals fall like soft-spoken sighs,
In colors bright, our passion lies.
Fluttering whispers in every hue,
   Desire dances, forever true.

In spring's embrace, love takes its ride,
Colors blending, with hearts as guide.
A canvas painted with gentle grace,
   In fluttering hues, we find our place.

The Space Between Us

In shadows cast by distant stars,
We find our whispers, soft and rare.
The space between is not so far,
A bridge of dreams where hearts can share.

Each sigh that dances on the breeze,
Connects our souls in silent ways.
Though miles apart, we're at ease,
In the realm where hope always stays.

Shimmers of Dreamlike Encounters

In twilight's glow, your laughter spark,
A fleeting moment, brief yet bright.
Each gaze exchanged ignites a mark,
An echo held in the soft night.

Our paths entwined in whispered fate,
Each chance encounter, a sweet chance.
In this dance of love, we create,
Memories that forever enhance.

Flickering Flames of Hidden Affection

Beneath the surface, feelings swell,
A flicker sparks, igniting heat.
In hushed glances, stories tell,
Of hearts entwined, a bond discreet.

Each secret glance, a burning flame,
A warmth that wraps the lonely night.
In silence, we play a sweet game,
Where love's flicker casts its light.

Heartbeats in Serendipitous Moments

In crowded rooms, our eyes align,
A spark ignites within the crowd.
The serendipity's design,
Brings heartbeats louder, proud and loud.

With each heartbeat, a chance unfolds,
A journey we were meant to take.
In moments brief, our story holds,
A tapestry that dreams make.

The Language of Silken Touch

In whispers soft, the silk will glide,
Across the skin, where secrets hide.
A tender breeze, like lovers lost,
Through gentle hands, we feel the cost.

Each thread of warmth, a tale untold,
Of passions deep, and hearts of gold.
With every brush, a spark ignites,
In silken touch, the soul delights.

Dancing Leaves of Emotive Reminiscence

Leaves swirl down, like memories fly,
In autumn's grace, they bid goodbye.
A crisp embrace, where colors blend,
Echoes of joy, they do not end.

Whispers of wind, through branches sway,
Invite the heart to dance and play.
In every twirl, a story's spun,
Of days gone by, of laughter's sun.

A Mosaic of Yearning Colors

In hues of dreams, the canvas glows,
A patchwork life, where longing flows.
With every stroke, emotions blaze,
A vibrant world, through myriad ways.

The heart, a palette, seeks to blend,
With shades of hope, it will transcend.
In each embrace, the colors merge,
A masterpiece of love's great urge.

The Gentle Lift of Unfulfilled Dreams

In twilight's hush, the dreams ascend,
On whispers light, they seek to mend.
A floating wish, on evening's sigh,
Through starry paths, they aim to fly.

Yet shadows dance, where doubts reside,
In gentle lifts, we turn the tide.
With every hope, a chance to soar,
To touch the sky, and dream once more.

Secrets in the Fluttering Sky

Whispers dance on gentle breeze,
Clouds hold tales of ancient seas.
Soft hues blend as day takes flight,
Stars emerge to greet the night.

Moonbeams spill on silent ground,
In the stillness, secrets found.
Each twinkle shares a hidden lore,
Of passions, dreams, and much more.

The sky, a canvas vast and wide,
Holds reflections, worlds inside.
In subtle shifts and colored beams,
Lie the echoes of our dreams.

When Thoughts Take Flight

Birds soar high in cerulean space,
Ideas spread with elegant grace.
Wings of wonder, hearts unbound,
In every thought, a spark is found.

Moments captured in the air,
Invisible threads, a silent prayer.
Chasing shadows, bright and slight,
When thoughts gather, they ignite.

Branches sway, the wind does sing,
A melody that hope will bring.
With every whisper, dreams take shape,
In every flight, a new escape.

Murmurs of an Untold Story

In corners dim, where shadows creep,
Lie stories buried, secrets deep.
Murmurs flicker like candlelight,
Igniting hearts in the still night.

Pages worn with tales untold,
Of dreams that shimmer, brave and bold.
Silent voices in the air,
Yearning for someone to care.

The past unfolds like petals bright,
Revealing truths hidden from sight.
In every sigh, a tale will find,
A way to bond and heal the blind.

Drifting Through Waves of Emotion

Tides of feelings rise and fall,
Waves of joy, a soothing call.
Pull of sorrow, pushing back,
In the depths, we feel the lack.

Ripples softly touch the shore,
Whispers linger evermore.
Seas of laughter, storms of doubt,
Through it all, we're finding out.

Sailing on this ocean vast,
Navigating through the past.
Balancing on waves we ride,
In the depths, we learn to hide.

Mosaics of Intertwined Hearts

In the silence where whispers play,
Two souls dance in a gentle sway.
Colors blend in love's embrace,
Mosaics form a sacred space.

Threads of laughter, tears combine,
Creating patterns, soft and fine.
Every shard a story told,
In this art, our hearts unfold.

Fading light as day departs,
Reflections echo, intertwined hearts.
Each fragment shines, a work of art,
Forever bound, we'll never part.

Each moment captured, shining bright,
Mosaics glow in the soft night light.
Hand in hand, we'll weave our fate,
In this tapestry, love won't wait.

Journey through the Fog of Desire

Into the mist where shadows creep,
Our secret wishes softly leap.
Whispers linger in murky air,
Yearning souls, stripped down, laid bare.

Paths entwined in ethereal gray,
Guided dreams lead us astray.
Every step a heartbeat's plea,
Lost in longing, you and me.

The fog thickens, time stands still,
Craving moments that thrill and chill.
In the haze, our spirits soar,
Each gaze a promise, forevermore.

As dawn breaks, the mist will part,
Revealing truths that pierce the heart.
Through the fog, our love will shine,
An endless journey, yours and mine.

Raindrops on a Canvas of Yearning

Raindrops fall like whispered dreams,
Painting love with gentle beams.
Each droplet holds a desire's sigh,
On this canvas, spirits fly.

Colors blend, the storm ignites,
In the chaos, love ignites.
Brushes stroke the hearts of fate,
Every splash, a chance to relate.

With every shower, wishes bloom,
In the tempest, dispelling gloom.
Yearning flows like rivers wide,
In this art, our hearts collide.

At twilight's edge, the skies will clear,
Revealing all we hold so dear.
Raindrops linger, a soft embrace,
On this canvas, we find our place.

Secrets Written in Starlight

Under the stars, secrets reside,
In the night where dreams abide.
Faint glimmers, a cosmic tale,
Whispers succeed, love will prevail.

Each star a wish, each wish a bond,
Threads of fate that wander beyond.
In velvet skies, our hopes align,
In starlit ink, our hearts entwine.

A constellation of tender sighs,
Mapping the love that never dies.
Each twinkle a promise we can keep,
In the shadows, our secrets seep.

With dawn's light, the stars will fade,
But in our hearts, the dreams are laid.
Written in starlight, forever bright,
Our love a journey, infinite flight.

Beneath the Veil of Uncertainty

In the twilight's gentle sigh,
Whispers linger, hopes comply.
Shadows dance with silent grace,
Navigating this uncertain space.

Dreams entwine with fears of night,
Casting flickers, fading light.
Beneath the veil, we seek the truth,
Chasing echoes of lost youth.

Clouds may gather, storms may brew,
Still, our hearts push ever through.
In the chaos, faith remains,
A steady pulse that breaks the chains.

So we march on, hand in hand,
In this ever-shifting land.
Beneath the veil, we find our way,
Embracing night, awaiting day.

Ephemeral Echoes of Longing

In the silence, a whisper calls,
Soft and sweet as daylight falls.
Yearning hearts in shadows stand,
Grasping dreams like grains of sand.

Moments fleeting, a breath, a sigh,
Stars that twinkle, then say goodbye.
Memories write in hearts' own ink,
Between the lines, we pause and think.

Like the tide that ebbs and flows,
Love's sweet current softly knows.
Connecting threads in twilight's hue,
Binding us, though time slips through.

In the distance, a soft refrain,
Carried on the gentle rain.
Within each echo, a love so bright,
Fleeting yet eternal light.

Threads of Delicate Affection

Woven tightly, soft and frail,
Life's sweet tapestry, we unveil.
Each thread whispers, stories blend,
Heartfelt moments, time won't end.

With tender hands, we stitch and weave,
Creating bonds that we believe.
In every knot, a promise tied,
In delicate safety, love abides.

Through golden hues of fading light,
We share our secrets, soft and bright.
Glimmers of joy in every seam,
Together, living out our dream.

As seasons change and shadows play,
Our threads will hold, come what may.
In every stitch, affection lives,
A tapestry that forever gives.

When Butterflies Dance in Shadows

In the garden, soft and still,
Butterflies flutter with gentle thrill.
Dancing lightly, casting mirth,
Whispers echo, heart to earth.

When shadows play beneath the trees,
Magic stirs in the evening breeze.
Delicate wings in twilight glow,
Carrying secrets only they know.

Each flutter tells a silent tale,
Of love's journey, gentle, frail.
Through petals soft, they twist and turn,
In the darkness, our hearts yearn.

As stars awaken in the night,
Butterflies dance, a fleeting sight.
Caught in dreams, we watch in awe,
Nature's beauty, a perfect law.

Love's Airy Labyrinth

In whispers soft, we find our way,
Through winding paths where shadows play.
Hearts entangled, secrets shared,
In love's embrace, we're truly bared.

A dance of flares, a silent song,
In this maze, we both belong.
Each turn reveals a brand new sight,
Together lost, yet filled with light.

The Flutter of Unvoiced Dreams

In corners dark where wishes hide,
A flutter stirs, as hearts collide.
Beneath the sky, so vast and wide,
These unvoiced dreams can't be denied.

Like fireflies in the night's embrace,
They twist and turn, a fleeting chase.
Each secret wish, a moment's gleam,
Together we weave our silent dream.

Glints of Emotion Amidst the Tumult

The storm may roar, but here we stand,
With glints of love, a steady hand.
In chaos loud, our hearts align,
In every glance, a spark divine.

Through crashing waves, we find our peace,
Amidst the noise, our joys increase.
With every pulse, as tempests swirl,
Our bond remains, forever unfurled.

A Palette of Fluttering Thoughts

Colors swirl in the mind's expanse,
Each thought a note in love's grand dance.
Brushstrokes soft on a canvas bright,
Fluttering dreams take graceful flight.

In hues of joy, and shades of pain,
We paint the moments, sun and rain.
A masterpiece etched in time's embrace,
A palette rich where our hearts trace.

Shimmering Hues of Anticipation

Golden rays of dawn arise,
Painting skies with soft surprise.
Whispers linger in the air,
Hopeful hearts, a vibrant flare.

Colors blend, a sight to see,
Dreams ignited, wild and free.
Moments spark like fireflies,
In the dusk, the magic lies.

Fingers reach for distant light,
Yearning for a future bright.
Promises beneath the stars,
Guiding us through life's sweet scars.

Chasing Shadows of Sensation

Footsteps echo, whispers near,
Chasing shadows, drawing near.
Every glance a soft caress,
In the dance, we find our rest.

Fleeting moments tease and play,
Silhouettes that fade away.
Crisp and cool the evening air,
Fleeting breath, we feel the care.

Laughter lingers, soft and warm,
In the calm, we find our charm.
Chasing dreams that softly fade,
In the night, our hearts invade.

Moments When Time Stands Still

Silent whispers, hearts aligned,
In a gaze, the world unwind.
Time suspends, the clock ignores,
In your eyes, eternity soars.

Gentle breezes, soft embrace,
In this scene, we find our place.
Every heartbeat, every sigh,
Captures life as moments fly.

Hold my hand, we'll drift away,
In the now, we choose to stay.
Moments cherished, etched in time,
In your presence, life's a rhyme.

The Dance of What Might Be

Twilight glimmers, hopes arise,
Dancing gently in the skies.
Steps we take, a rhythmic flow,
Guided by a world to know.

Fate entwines with every beat,
In the dark, our dreams repeat.
Each new turn, a chance to see,
What awaits in mystery.

Winds of change, they call us near,
In the silence, dreams appear.
Dare to dream, embrace the night,
In the dance, we find our light.

Euphoria of Sudden Connections

In a crowded room, eyes meet,
A spark ignites, electric heat.
Laughter dances in the air,
Strangers drawn, a moment rare.

Words flow freely, hearts collide,
In this moment, we confide.
Time seems to halt, a blissful trance,
Two souls caught in a fleeting dance.

Promises whispered, futures bright,
Under stars that gleam with light.
In shared glances, secrets bloom,
Euphoria breaks the silent gloom.

As dawn approaches, shadows fade,
Yet memories of joy cascade.
Though paths may part, hearts remain,
In the echo of love's refrain.

The Breath Between Heartbeats

In stillness holds a gentle pause,
A moment cherished, just because.
Time slows down, the world outside,
In breaths exchanged, our hearts collide.

With every sigh, the universe speaks,
A silence vibrant, all it seeks.
In the hush, emotions swell,
Each heartbeat tells a story well.

The space between is rich and vast,
In whispers soft, the die is cast.
A delicate dance, two souls in blend,
In breaths held close, we transcend.

Each heartbeat echoes with desire,
Filling the void, igniting fire.
In this silence, we find our way,
Through the breath that longs to stay.

Night-Time Reveries of Longing

Beneath the moon, shadows creep,
Whispers stir from dreams we keep.
In the dark, hearts start to yearn,
For absent love, a steady burn.

Stars above hold secrets tight,
Guiding thoughts in endless night.
In every sigh, a wish takes flight,
To bridge the gap 'tween dark and light.

The clock strikes softly, echoes fade,
Memories linger, love portrayed.
In midnight's realm, time stands still,
Longing grows, a silent thrill.

With every heartbeat, chances missed,
In reveries, we find our bliss.
Longing dances through the air,
In night's embrace, we dream and dare.

Flickers of Hope in Quiet Dusk

As the sun dips low, shadows grow,
Flickers of hope begin to glow.
In twilight's calm, we find our grace,
Every heart seeks a warm embrace.

The world slows down, a gentle breath,
In quiet dusk, we dance with death.
Yet in the stillness, sparks ignite,
Promising dreams take flight tonight.

Stars peek out, a tender spark,
Painting the sky with dreams to embark.
In shadows deep, a flicker shines,
Guiding us through the darkest lines.

As night unfolds, we hold it dear,
In flickers of hope, we conquer fear.
For even as the light may fade,
In dusk's embrace, new paths are laid.

Whispers of Unseen Wings

In the quiet of the night,
Soft murmurs take their flight.
Gentle wings brush the air,
Whispers echo everywhere.

Shadows dance in the moon's embrace,
Promises linger, leaving trace.
A world beyond the visible hue,
Where dreams and secrets softly grew.

Every sigh tells a story deep,
Guarded tales that shadows keep.
In stillness, the heart takes wing,
As unseen voices softly sing.

Beyond the stars, hope glows bright,
Guiding souls through endless night.
In every whisper, a chance to find,
The unseen love that binds mankind.

Emotions on the Breeze

Fleeting thoughts like petals drift,
Carried on the wind's soft lift.
Whispers of love and grief intertwine,
In the gentle sway of summertime.

Each breeze brings a vivid hue,
A melody known to me and you.
Tender sighs on the cool air rise,
Echoing dreams woven with ties.

Moments lost in the winds of change,
Hearts awaken, feelings exchange.
In every gust, emotions soar,
Painting colors forevermore.

Like laughter caught in sunlit rays,
Floating freely through summer days.
Capture the whispers, hold them near,
Emotions dance, forever clear.

Tangles of Heartstrings in Flight

In the twilight's gentle embrace,
Heartstrings weave a tender trace.
With every beat, a story spins,
Tangles of love, where hope begins.

A symphony of souls in tune,
Dancing lightly 'neath the moon.
Each note sings of moments shared,
In the tapestry of lives laid bare.

Like feathers caught on the breath of fate,
Heartstrings flutter, never late.
Bound by dreams, the journey's fleet,
In tangled knots, our hearts do meet.

Together we rise, together we glide,
Through the currents, hearts open wide.
In the flight of love's sweet refrain,
Tangled together, we face the rain.

Secrets of a Swaying Heart

Beneath the willows, whispers weave,
Secrets that the shadows cleave.
A heart sways gently, lost in thought,
In the quiet, lessons sought.

With every rustle of the leaves,
Truths emerge, while the spirit grieves.
Swaying softly, the heart confides,
In the embrace where love abides.

Each heartbeat carries tales untold,
In every rhythm, a heart of gold.
Secrets woven in the breeze,
Lost in twilight, finding ease.

In the hush, a soft refrain,
Love's tender dance, joy and pain.
Secrets flourish in the dark,
Filling the night with a hopeful spark.

The Enigma of Fleeting Glances

In a crowded room, our eyes collide,
A moment stolen, where secrets hide.
With whispers soft, the silence sings,
Two souls entwined, the thrill it brings.

A glance that lingers, a heart that stirs,
An unspoken bond, in the air it blurs.
Each fluttered breath, a dance of fate,
In fleeting glances, we create our state.

A flicker of hope, a spark of fire,
In simple gazes, we share desire.
What lies ahead, remains unknown,
In shared glances, we find our home.

But like the breeze, they slip away,
These moments pass, but hearts will stay.
In memories bright, the echoes play,
The enigma lingers, come what may.

A Tangle of Heartstrings

In shadows cast where love resides,
A tangle of heartstrings, where joy collides.
Each note we play, a tender sound,
In the symphony of love, our hearts are bound.

Though trials come to test the bond,
In the chaos, there's something fond.
A gentle touch, a knowing glance,
In tangled chaos, we find our dance.

Whispered dreams on the edge of night,
We weave our hopes in soft twilight.
Through every storm, our spirits rise,
In the tangle, love never dies.

So let us hold, these heartstrings tight,
In the tapestry of day and night.
With every beat, we write our song,
Together as one, where we belong.

The Path of Unraveled Desires

Upon the path where dreams collide,
Unraveled desires, we cannot hide.
With every step, a choice to make,
In the dance of life, hearts will quake.

The stars above, a guiding light,
In shadows deep, they shine so bright.
Each twist and turn, a lesson learned,
As passions rise, our spirits burned.

We walk with purpose, through doubts and fears,
In the whispers of joy, we shed our tears.
With open hearts, we dare to seek,
In the silence, our souls will speak.

So take my hand, let's brave the night,
On this path of dreams, in love's pure flight.
Together we'll unravel what lies ahead,
In the journey of hopes, we'll be led.

Secrets in the Spaces Between

In silence shared, where words retreat,
Secrets linger in time's heartbeat.
A glance, a sigh, unspoken fears,
The spaces between hold hidden tears.

With every breath, a tale unfolds,
In quiet corners, our truth beholds.
The weight of dreams, both light and dark,
In stillness woven, we leave our mark.

In the pause of laughter, the hush of night,
Our stories echo in soft twilight.
What lies beneath, a tender ache,
In the in-between, we dare to wake.

So hold me close, as shadows fall,
In the gaps of silence, we hear the call.
For in these secrets, our spirits blend,
In the spaces between, love has no end.

The Allure of Unexplained Emotions

Whispers dance on silent nights,
Where shadows play with fleeting light.
A heart that skips, a lilted beat,
Unseen threads that tie, yet retreat.

Tangled thoughts that weave and spin,
A maze where none can truly win.
Each glance a puzzle, each sigh a clue,
In this labyrinth, I'm lost with you.

Emotions rise like tides at sea,
Pulling gently, then setting free.
The allure of what's left unsaid,
A book of dreams that stays unread.

In midnight's glow, the truth confides,
A fragile bridge where hope resides.
Let mystery guide us, sweet and wild,
For in the unknown, I'm still your child.

Bubbles of Hidden Affection

Tiny bursts, a secret smile,
Moments cherished, all the while.
Bubbles rising, soft and bright,
In quiet corners, pure delight.

Words unspoken, glances shared,
In every heartbeat, love declared.
A gentle touch, a fleeting spark,
Illuminates the hidden dark.

Dances in the depth of eyes,
Where truth resides, and passion flies.
Every heartbeat, every sigh,
A symphony, a whispered 'why.'

Like soft rain on thirsty ground,
In these bubbles, joy is found.
Together we float, light as air,
In a world where love lays bare.

Wings of a Questioning Heart

Fluttering softly in the breeze,
A heart that wonders, seeks to please.
Questions linger, answers hide,
In the depths, where fears reside.

Chasing dreams, a hesitant flight,
Through tangled paths, out of sight.
Each flutter whispers tales untold,
Of courage found and hearts bold.

With each beat, uncertainty sings,
The thrill of what tomorrow brings.
Wings that yearn for skies unknown,
In the journey, seeds are sown.

Yet still, I linger with delight,
For in the quest, there's purest light.
So let the winds guide my way,
With every question, hope's bouquet.

Constellations of Uncertain Feelings

Stars collide in midnight skies,
Mapping out the heart's goodbyes.
Constellations formed in doubt,
To understand what love's about.

Flickering lights, a cosmic dance,
Each twinkle offers a second chance.
In the vastness, I lose my way,
Navigating through night and day.

The sky whispers secrets, divine,
Connecting moments, yours and mine.
Yet shadows linger, softly weep,
In the night where dreams still sleep.

Awash in hues of dark and light,
Uncertain feelings take their flight.
Together we roam, hand in hand,
Mapping love's vast, uncharted land.

Enchanted by Fleeting Moments

In whispers soft as morning dew,
Time dances lightly, fleeting too.
Each glance a spark, a treasure rare,
We hold them close, suspended air.

Moments linger, then they fade,
Like shadows cast in light's parade.
Yet in our hearts, they brightly gleam,
A tapestry of endless dream.

We chase the hours, they slip away,
In gentle sighs, we often stray.
But in their wake, we find our grace,
Enchanted by this timeless space.

Chasing Rainbows of Emotion

Beneath the sky, a colors' dance,
Each hue a whisper, a fleeting chance.
We reach for joy, in storms we find,
The beauty woven, heart entwined.

With every tear, a layer peels,
Revealing depth, the soul reveals.
In laughter's light, the colors spark,
Chasing the rainbows through the dark.

Each memory gathers like the mist,
Holding the warmth we can't resist.
Emotions flow, a vibrant stream,
In every heart, a precious dream.

Echoes in the Twilight Air

As daylight fades, the night draws near,
Soft echoes linger, whispers clear.
In twilight's arms, the world turns slow,
A gentle hush, where shadows grow.

Silvered stars in velvet sky,
Hold secrets lost, where dreams may lie.
Each rustle speaks in hushed refrain,
An ancient song, a sweet, soft pain.

We listen close to the fading light,
In echoes found, our hearts take flight.
Together we share this tender hour,
The magic wrapped in twilight's power.

The Art of Halting Hearts

In fleeting glances, sparks ignite,
A world suspended, pure delight.
With every touch, our pulses race,
The art of halting time and space.

With breathless words, we carve the night,
Drawing close, a shared twilight.
Each heartbeat sings a love unknown,
In silence deep, we find our tone.

We hold the moment, tightly bound,
In whispers soft, our souls surround.
For in this dance, we find our part,
The wondrous art of halting hearts.

A Feather's Fall

A feather drifts through autumn air,
Lightly dancing without a care.
It whispers secrets to the breeze,
Carrying dreams with gentle ease.

From treetops high it takes its leap,
Into the world so vast and deep.
A soft descent on nature's quilt,
Where hopes and wishes softly wilt.

Each flutter tells of space and time,
Of fleeting moments that once chimed.
In every turn, a story spun,
Of all that's lost and all that's won.

In its stillness, life unfolds,
A tale of peace, of warmth, of gold.
The feather's fall is nature's art,
A timeless journey, heart to heart.

A Heart's Rise

A heart awakens in the dawn,
With dreams of love, a joyful song.
It beats with hope, a steady drum,
In every pulse, new chances come.

Through shadows past and whispers meek,
It finds the strength to softly speak.
A rise like sun in morning light,
Illuminating dark with bright.

With every step, a courage grows,
A garden where affection flows.
It learns to trust, it learns to feel,
In tender moments, love is real.

When hearts collide, the magic's clear,
A dance of souls, drawing near.
To rise anew with each embrace,
In love's warm glow, a sacred space.

The Embrace of Unexpressed Feelings

In silence linger words unspoken,
A heavy weight, a heart that's broken.
The feelings dwell beneath the skin,
A battle fought, a war within.

Each glance a ghost of what could be,
A fleeting thought, a memory.
The longing pools in every sigh,
A wish to soar, to never die.

Yet still we stand, a frozen dance,
In shadows cast by fleeting chance.
The words we crave, they hide away,
In secret spaces, they long to play.

To open up is to let go,
To feel the warmth of what we know.
In the embrace, the silence bends,
Where unexpressed love finally mends.

Butterflies Beneath the Surface

Beneath the waves, where whispers hide,
A dance of colors, bright and wide.
The butterflies of ocean's heart,
In currents swift, they play their part.

With gentle grace, they rise and fall,
In silent beauty, they enthrall.
Their wings a tapestry of dreams,
Beneath the surface, life redeems.

In shadows cast by sunlight's glow,
They flutter soft, they ebb, they flow.
A hidden world, a secret song,
Where nature's wonders all belong.

To see them dance beneath the waves,
Is to believe in what love saves.
With every stroke, their beauty gleams,
In quiet realms, they chase their dreams.

When Curiosity Ignites

A spark of wonder in the night,
When questions swirl and minds take flight.
The world unfolds in shades of bright,
As curiosity ignites.

From tiny seeds, great stories bloom,
Each mystery dispels the gloom.
With every glance, new tales arise,
In boundless realms, the spirit flies.

To seek, to wander, to explore,
To find the keys to life's locked door.
The thrill of questing in the dark,
When curiosity leaves its mark.

With each discovery, hearts expand,
In knowledge held within our hands.
For when we seek, we truly see,
The beauty in what's yet to be.

The Enchantment of Fluttered Souls

In gardens where the whispers play,
The petals dance, then drift away.
Each color bursts with silent glee,
A tapestry of dreams set free.

Upon the breeze, a soft refrain,
Two hearts entwined, a sweet disdain.
The moonlight casts its silver glow,
As secrets shared begin to flow.

They stroll through shadows, hand in hand,
While stars above like wishes stand.
With every pulse, a magic spark,
Their laughter echoes through the dark.

In fleeting moments lost in time,
Their souls embrace in tender rhyme.
With every glance, a promise told,
In whispers soft, their love unfolds.

Ephemeral Passions in the Air

Beneath the sky where tempests rise,
Two hearts collide, a sweet surprise.
In stolen glances, fire ignites,
A dance of fate on moonlit nights.

Each breath shared whispers like a song,
In fleeting time, where lovers throng.
With every touch, the world suspends,
As laughter lingers and joy transcends.

Yet seasons change, the winds will shift,
A fragile bond, a fleeting gift.
In shadows cast by moments past,
They chase the dawn, their love steadfast.

In dreams they twirl, the stars align,
With echoes soft, their hearts entwine.
An ephemeral glimpse of the divine,
In passion's air, their souls combine.

Chasing Shadows of Heartfelt Whimsy

Through fields of gold, where shadows fall,
They chase the whimsy, heed the call.
With laughter bright as sunlight beams,
In every step, they weave their dreams.

A fluttered heart, a whispered sigh,
They dance beneath the vast blue sky.
In playful glances, mischief reigns,
While time slows down and love remains.

As twilight drapes the world in hue,
Their spirits soar, both fresh and new.
With every heartbeat, laughter spills,
In fleeting moments, love fulfills.

They chase the shadows, run afar,
Across the meadows, guided by stars.
In woven tales of whimsy bright,
They find their home in love's pure light.

Breaths of Love Amidst the Leaves

In autumn's grasp, where colors blend,
They find a quiet place to mend.
With every rustle, love takes flight,
In whispered secrets, soft and light.

Underneath the ancient trees,
They breathe in love, a gentle breeze.
With every laugh, the world stands still,
In tender moments, hearts do fill.

The leaves cascade, a golden rain,
Each flutter echoes joy and pain.
With hands entwined, their dreams grow loud,
As nature weaves a silent shroud.

In twilight's glow, they share a sigh,
While starlit wishes float on high.
In every breath, a promise stays,
Amidst the leaves, love finds its ways.

The Dance of Hesitant Hearts

In twilight's hush, we find our way,
Hearts abloom, yet shy to sway.
With trembling steps, we start the dance,
In this moment, a fleeting chance.

Voices soft like whispered dreams,
Unraveled hope, or so it seems.
Each glance a spark, igniting fears,
A rhythm swells, drowned in tears.

Fingers touch, then pull away,
What do words dare not convey?
In every twirl, a silent plea,
To break the chains, of you and me.

Yet in the dark, we still will sway,
Two hesitant hearts, come what may.
In the dance of shadows, we'll confide,
No longer strangers, side by side.

Kaleidoscope of Yearning

Colors burst in vibrant hues,
Each spin reveals a different view.
Yearning hearts, a fleeting thrill,
Chasing dreams, forever still.

Through prisma light, we find our way,
A symphony of night and day.
In patterns woven, tales unfold,
Whispers of love, both timid and bold.

Fractured moments, soft and bright,
Scattered hopes, a fragile flight.
Each fragment whispers secrets past,
A kaleidoscope, forever cast.

Yet still we seek, though lost in time,
In every shade, a silent rhyme.
From dusk to dawn, our spirits soar,
In longing's light, forevermore.

Captured by a Soft Breeze

A gentle touch upon my skin,
The world slows down, the dance begins.
Sweet whispers carried through the air,
With every sigh, I feel you there.

Dancing leaves, they swirl and sway,
In nature's grasp, we find our way.
The breeze, a serenade so fine,
It holds the love that feels like wine.

In subtle notes of rustling trees,
Your laughter lingers with the breeze.
Each flutter brings your spirit near,
In every breath, I taste your fear.

Yet in this moment, time stands still,
A soft embrace, a sweetened thrill.
We chase the whispers, not the past,
Captured by a breeze, forever cast.

Fluttering Fragments of Truth

Scattered leaves in autumn's dance,
Each one tells a tale of chance.
Fluttering softly through the air,
Fragments of truth are everywhere.

With every breeze, a story shared,
Of hidden dreams and hearts laid bare.
In the rustle, secrets lie,
Whispers of love that never die.

We gather pieces from the ground,
In their embrace, we are unbound.
A puzzle made of hopes and fears,
Fluttering fragments through the years.

Yet in this chaos, beauty lies,
In every truth, we realize.
Though scattered wide, our hearts remain,
Connected still, through joy and pain.

Fleeting Words on a Gentle Breeze

In the twilight's soft embrace,
Words echo, lost in time.
Carried forth on whispers light,
Like petals kissed by prime.

Tales of laughter, fleeting grace,
Dance upon the air.
They linger for a moment's warmth,
Then vanish, unaware.

Each story wraps around the heart,
A gentle, fleeting sigh.
They stir the soul, igniting dreams,
Then float away and fly.

Yet in the depth of silence,
Their essence lingers near.
For every word once spoken,
Leaves traces, crystal clear.

A Nebula of Uncertain Affections

In shadows deep, where feelings swell,
A nebula of doubt does bloom.
Uncertain hearts in silent night,
Drift softly, lost in gloom.

Amidst the stars of hope and fear,
A spark ignites, then fades away.
Caught in the dance of what might be,
We long for words to stay.

Through swirling mist of dreams untold,
We search for clarity's embrace.
Yet love, like stardust, slips our hands,
A fleeting, ethereal trace.

In cosmic depths, emotions twist,
A tapestry of what we crave.
Yet every heartbeat maps the void,
A journey we shall brave.

The Labyrinth of Unvoiced Love

In shadows cast by unspoken stakes,
Love hides in corners deep.
A labyrinth where silence reigns,
Secrets we dare not keep.

With every glance, a story waits,
In twisting paths we roam.
Yet words, like strands of golden thread,
Weave tales that lead us home.

Each heartbeat echoes in the dark,
A map of what could be.
Though lost in folds of timid hearts,
Hope whispers courage free.

In this maze of tangled minds,
True feelings softly blend.
For love that dares to stay untold,
Can still transcend, my friend.

Fleeting Whispers on the Wind

Whispers float on evening's breath,
Soft secrets shared in flight.
Like autumn leaves that sway and twirl,
They vanish in the night.

Moments captured, bittersweet,
Dance upon the breeze.
They linger long, yet fade away,
Like ripples on the seas.

Each sigh a mark of memories,
That time cannot reclaim.
For whispers, like the fleeting stars,
Are shadows without name.

Yet in the silence left behind,
Echoes find their place.
For every whisper on the wind,
Leaves traces we embrace.

The Butterfly Effect of Unsung Words

Whispers dance on the evening air,
Soft notes lost in gentle despair.
Each syllable, a fluttering wing,
Creating ripples that softly cling.

A story untold, yet felt so deep,
In the silence, secrets we keep.
Echoes fade, but the impact stays,
A symphony woven in tender ways.

In hearts bound by unspoken dreams,
The smallest gestures burst at the seams.
Like petals drifting from bloom's embrace,
They shape our world with subtle grace.

With every thought left unexpressed,
A fragile truth hangs, a silent quest.
For every word that goes unheard,
A universe shifts with unsung word.

Unraveling the Fabric of Yearning

Threads of longing weave through the night,
In shadows cast, hopes take flight.
Silken dreams wrapped in desire,
Each pulse ignites an inner fire.

Time drifts softly on whispering winds,
A tapestry where longing begins.
Every stitch a delicate tale,
Woven with love, never to pale.

Fingers trace where heartbeats race,
A journey mapped in every space.
Glimmers of promise unfurl and sway,
Unraveling paths that lead us astray.

Yet in the fabric of fate, we find,
A mirror held to the yearnings entwined.
Each thread connects, a cosmic art,
In the tapestry of a yearning heart.

Footsteps on the Edge of Desire

Echoes whisper where shadows meet,
Footsteps linger in rhythm's beat.
On the edge, a line softly drawn,
Between the dusk and the break of dawn.

Each desire, a spark in the dark,
Guiding us where the flames leave a mark.
A delicate dance on uncertain ground,
Where dreams awaken and hope is found.

Fingers grazing on velvet night,
Chasing visions of passion's light.
With hearts aflame, we reach for more,
On the brink where desires pour.

Together we tread, this fragile line,
With every breath, our souls entwine.
In the twilight's embrace, we'll find our way,
With footsteps echoing what hearts say.

Harmonies of the Heart's Search

In the stillness, a melody flows,
Seeking the truth that the heart knows.
Each note a whisper, a soft caress,
Guiding us through love's wilderness.

Voices blend in a tender hum,
In the chorus of love, we're yet to come.
A symphony crafted in silence and song,
Drawing us close where we both belong.

Waves of longing crash on the shore,
Ebbing and flowing, craving for more.
Each heartbeat echoes the rhythm divine,
In the dance of our souls, forever entwined.

As dusk turns to stars, we softly weave,
The harmonies born of all we believe.
In the love's embrace, where dreams ignite,
We'll find our way in the serenade night.

Whirlwinds of Unvoiced Dreams

In shadows deep, where whispers fade,
Soft secrets stir, in silence laid.
The heartbeats echo, stifled screams,
Unraveled threads of unvoiced dreams.

Hoisted high, on fate's cruel wheel,
Desires rise, yet none can feel.
The tempest swirls, yet lost we roam,
In whirlwinds vast, we find no home.

Beneath the stars, our hopes ignite,
Yet clouds obscure the path to light.
With every gust, we twist and bend,
Chasing storms that never end.

A dance of wishes, soft and bright,
We wade through dusk, in search of night.
In every spin, there's truth concealed,
A tapestry of dreams revealed.

Tides of Transient Passion

Upon the shore, our hearts collide,
In fleeting waves, we must abide.
The sun sets low, the colors bleed,
In tides of passion, we plant the seed.

Emotions crash like ocean spray,
A moment's spark in wild array.
With every surge, the thrill expands,
We dance entwined on shifting sands.

Yet time's embrace pulls us away,
As echoes of our laughter sway.
The moonlit tides may ebb and flow,
But passion's fire can still bestow.

In remnants left, our spirits fly,
A fleeting love, not meant to die.
In dreams we'll meet, where hearts convene,
In waves of passion, forever keen.

Language of Wandering Souls

Across the night, our voices roam,
In whispers soft, we seek our home.
With every step, a tale untold,
The language blooms, in hearts of gold.

In shadows cast, we share our fears,
The silent truths, the hidden years.
Through distant lands, our spirits chase,
The universal, warm embrace.

A symphony of souls we weave,
In every laugh, a chance to grieve.
Yet as we wander, bonds grow tight,
In the woven threads of shared light.

Together long, together wide,
In search of meaning, side by side.
The language forged, forever whole,
A map of love for every soul.

Fading Footprints of What-ifs

In misty dawn, our footprints fade,
Each step a choice, a price we paid.
The echoes linger, soft and low,
In fading light, our dreams may go.

What if the roads had turned askew?
What if our hearts had wholly knew?
Regrets will whisper, secrets stir,
In shadows cast, our voices purr.

Yet in the sands, new paths shall rise,
With every tide, the sun complies.
In what-ifs held, there's room to find,
A brighter fate, a life unlined.

So take a step beyond the lost,
And cherish love, despite the cost.
In fading footprints, hope still sways,
To guide our hearts through endless ways.

The Harmonies of Howling Desire

In shadows where our secrets meet,
The echoes dance beneath our feet.
A whisper soft, a fleeting glance,
In every touch, a wild romance.

The moonlit sky, our silent stage,
As passions rise, we turn the page.
Each heartbeat sings a lover's song,
In harmonies where we belong.

With every breath, the night ignites,
Desires blaze in stolen nights.
Through tangled dreams, we find our way,
In the symphony of night and day.

Together bound, we chase the fire,
Through every storm, our hearts conspire.
In the ebb and flow of chance,
We dance in the flames of sweet romance.

Flights of Fancy on a Summer Breeze

Beneath a sky of azure hue,
Where wildflowers dance, and dreams come true.
We chase the whispers of the wind,
On summer's breath, our souls rescind.

In laughter light as drifting clouds,
With secrets shared beneath the crowds.
We weave our tales in golden light,
In flights of fancy, hearts take flight.

The gentle warmth of sunlit days,
Guides us through a fragrant maze.
Adventures await in every sigh,
As breezes lift, and spirits fly.

With every turn, new paths we find,
In the tapestry of hearts entwined.
As summer wanes, our memories freeze,
In the timeless dance of the summer breeze.

Caresses of Hidden Longing

Beneath the surface, silence speaks,
In secret glances, longing seeks.
A brush of skin, a fleeting touch,
In whispered dreams, we crave so much.

The shadows hold our hidden fears,
In silent nights, we shed our tears.
Through yearning eyes, our hearts collide,
In the caresses where hopes reside.

A stolen moment, a stolen breath,
In quiet corners, we flirt with death.
With every sigh, our souls align,
In the delicate dance of the divine.

Though distance grows and time may part,
These hidden longings fill the heart.
In echoes soft, we still remain,
In every whisper, love's sweet pain.

The Undercurrent of Starlit Night

Across the sky, the stars align,
In whispered tales where dreams entwine.
The night unfolds its velvet shroud,
In silken shadows, we're allowed.

With every glimmer, secrets flow,
The uncharted paths we dare to go.
In constellations, wishes soar,
Beyond the waves of distant shores.

In the depths of night, we find the truth,
With every heartbeat, we reclaim our youth.
The undercurrent pulls us near,
In starlit sighs, our fears disappear.

Together lost in cosmic grace,
We find our place in time and space.
With every dream that takes its flight,
We dance beneath the starlit night.

The Flight of Fleeting Wishes

Wishes glide through the night's soft air,
Whispers of dreams, light as a prayer.
Carried on winds, they dance and weave,
In the heart's cradle, they softly cleave.

Like butterflies caught in a sunny ray,
They flit and flutter, then drift away.
A kaleidoscope of hopes set free,
In the silence, we yearn to see.

Yet still they linger, just out of reach,
Lessons of longing, their quiet speech.
Each moment lost carries a song,
In the shadows where wishes belong.

And as they vanish into the night,
We hold them close, in dim candlelight.
Fleeting whispers, never quite found,
In the breathless stillness, dreams abound.

A Tapestry Woven with Breathless Hope

Threads of gold in the dusk return,
Every stitch a flicker, a flame that burns.
Woven with secrets, dreams intertwined,
A fabric of moments, tenderly aligned.

Silk and linen, the colors define,
Each heart's wish in a gentle line.
Breathless hope fills the spaces between,
In whispers of joy, quietly seen.

Stories unfold in a delicate gaze,
Each pattern reflects the wind's soft blaze.
A canvas painted in shadows and light,
Breathless hopes in the deepening night.

While time weaves on with a passionate hand,
Stitches of longing across the land.
In this tapestry, we find our way,
A map of our hearts, come what may.

Reflections of a Dappled Heart

In the garden where sunlight plays,
Dappled light in a myriad of ways.
Shadows dance on the petals dear,
Soft whispers echo, drawing near.

Each heartbeat resonates with the breeze,
In the rustle of leaves, a gentle tease.
A reflection of love in the rippling pond,
Ripples of memories, forever fond.

The colors blend in a tender embrace,
Moments captured in time and space.
Dappled hearts hold both joy and pain,
In a symphony sung in the rain.

As twilight descends, the echoes remain,
Chasing shadows, we break from the chain.
Reflections shimmer in dusk's soft light,
Guiding lost souls into the night.

Wings Heavy with Unspoken Words

Wings that tremble, with secrets they bear,
Heavy with want, they hang in the air.
Each flutter a pause, a sigh in the breeze,
Unspoken words, they beg to be released.

Like feathers fallen from a weeping dove,
Tangled in hopes, lost whispers of love.
Burdened by stories that never took flight,
In the longing, they hide from the light.

Stars dimmed by thoughts we cannot convey,
Echoes trapped in the night's soft sway.
Their silence screams louder than any call,
Wings heavy, perhaps, to rise at all.

Yet still they dream of the skies above,
Yearning to soar, to find peace in love.
For in stillness, the heart knows the way,
To whisper the truths of yesterday.

Milton Keynes UK
Ingram Content Group UK Ltd.
UKHW021938121124
451129UK00007B/134